The Winds' Child

Mark Taylor

ILLUSTRATED BY
Erik Blegvad

Atheneum   1973   New York

To Shirley, Hal, Laurie, and David
Who heard it first one summer day
Long past, yet never far away.

The Winds' Child

How the Story Began

Once a kitten lived all alone in a tree of pine.

A witch Wind came howling through the branches
   dark.
Well—
This is the Winds' Child's story to tell.

"*A Winds' Child Wild and Lonely*"

Black as the cat I am,
On another day, a long ago day,
I lived alone in a tree of pine.

I had certain friends:
Daytime friends and *nighttime* friends.
The four winds were my daytime friends.
The moon and stars were my nighttime friends.
But they were friends that came and went,
Never to stay.

I was called the Winds' Child,
Because I knew what the four winds said.
White Wind of the North rattled the needles of my
   tree of pine
And talked of things cold.

Blue Wind of the East rustled through the tall grass
And talked of things wet.

Gold Wind of the South hummed on summer evenings
And talked of things sunny.

Grey Wind of the West skimmed across the water of the pond
And talked of things far away.

The four winds were my friends.

One day I asked them, "From where did I come?"

And the four winds said, "Better to ask us where are
   you going?"

And then I asked, "Why am I lonely?"

And they blew softly, "Winds are never lonely.

Are you not a Winds' Child?

Be wild!"

"The Owl's Questions"

Then my neighbor owl spoke to me one night and
   said,
"Winds' Child, what is your heart's desire?"
"Not to be lonely!" I cried.
   But the owl replied, "Are you not wild?"
   And when I answered, "Must wild be lonely?"
   He only stared at the stars till morning.

Then another night neighbor owl stared at me and
    said,
"Your heart's desire is to find a friend
  Who will not come and go
  Like winds, and stars, and moon.
"Another friend?" I asked. "But where?"
"Not where," he said, "but who?"

Who would be another friend?
I asked the moon and stars.
The moon hung like a lamp above my tree of pine.
"Who is my heart's desire?" asked I.
The stars crackled above me high.
"Where is another friend?" called I,
"A friend to stay?"

One day I asked the four winds to help me find
    my heart's desire.
"Who told you of it?" said they.
"The owl," said I, "said who?"
"I can help you find only green juniper berries in
    the snow,"
Said White Wind.

"I will bring you secret scents from beyond the hills,"
Said Blue Wind.

"I will help you find golden pears, warm in the sun,"
Said Gold Wind.

"I can show you silver fish asleep in silver pools,"
Said Grey Wind.
But these were not my heart's desire.
They were not a friend to stay,
Never to go away.

"The Witch Wind's Answers"

And then the Witch Wind came one night,
Black as the cat I am,
And cried, "Where? Where? Where?"
Until my tree of pine sighed, "Here! Here! Here!"
The Witch Wind screamed, "There? There!"
Until I was stiff-furred with wonder.
And my neighbor owl cried,
"Who? Who? Who?"
The moon smiled at me.
"You," I thought she said.
And the pin-pointed stars, like bell sounds,
Twinkled, "Look! Look! Look!"

The Witch Wind rustled my fur
And hollered, "Child! Child! Child!"
I did not know what the Witch Wind meant.
For the Witch Wind was black as the cat I am,
Sharp as the claws of my feet,
Secret as the thoughts in my eyes,
Wise as my whiskers.
"Come with me!" the Witch Wind cried.
"Black as the cat you are, come with me!"
But I was afraid.

I stayed in my tree of pine.
I played with the four winds.
North Wind showed me white frost on the ground.
North Wind was cold and stiffened my whiskers.
East Wind blew grey clouds through the sky
And scattered silver raindrops for me to chase.

South Wind brought golden butterflies
To dance around my tree of pine.
West Wind brought soft, sweet smells
And rubbed them in my fur.
But they were friends to come and go,
Never to stay
Nor make me purr.

But another night the Witch Wind scratched upon my
    tree of pine
And said, "I know where to find your heart's desire!"
The moon, yellow and fat, seemed to say, "Go!"
And neighbor owl cried, "Who!"
I came down from my tree of pine.
I followed the Witch Wind.
How we ran, black as the cat I am!
We ran where the Witch Wind tugged and pushed.
Out of the forest we ran, around the pond,
Through the field,
To the hill beyond.

"Come! Run! Where? There!" the Witch Wind cried.
But I was lost and cold.
Gone was my tree of pine.
Gone was the pond.
Gone were the fields I knew.

The moon still hung and swung in the sky.
And the far-away stars were tingling high.
And the Witch Wind's cry was, "There!
Another friend is there!"
And then I saw a thing called House.

A great pumpkin face sat in the window,
Grinning, grinning, grinning
At me, black as the cat I am,
Making me tired, making me cold.
This was not another friend,
This was not my heart's desire.
The Witch Wind rattled the shutters,
And scuffed the leaves, and slapped the leaves
    against the window
Where the pumpkin face was grinning, grinning.
Rattle and scuff, grin and shake!
"Halloweeeeeen!" screeched the Witch Wind.
"Halloweeeeeen!" shrieked the Witch Wind.

"A Girl Named Who"

The door opened.
It was filled with light—so bright!
"Who's there?" someone asked the night.
And the owl flew high above shouting, "Who!"
And a voice replied, "That's me.
I'm Who."

It was a girl
With hair black as the cat I am.
She looked at me and laughed.
"Cat," she said,
"I heard you there!
I heard the Witch Wind too,
Howling on the air."

"Halloween!" shrieked the Witch Wind.

I hollered, too.

But the girl said, "Hush.

Don't be wild."

"Will you run?" shrieked the Witch Wind,

"Will you run, Winds' Child?"

But the girl said, "Stay,

Don't be wild."

And touched my fur with a gentle hand,

And said again, "Oh, stay."

What should I do?

She said, "Stay."

She was Who.

But the Witch Wind hollered, "Will you run

    away?"

And then I knew what the Witch Wind knew:

I should not run.

"I will stay," I hollered.

And the Witch Wind laughed.

Then, black as the cat I am,

She scattered all her ragged clouds from sight

And left the night all quiet with stars.

Who held me.
Others came.
"He is the Winds' Child," said Who.
"He's only a stray," said they.
But Who replied, "The Witch Wind brought him
     here to stay,
To be my friend,
Black as the cat he is."

So the owl was right,
And Who is my heart's desire.
When there is time,
I show her my moon and my stars,
And tell her of the four winds,
And take her to my tree of pine.
She loves them, too, and says,
"I know, Winds' Child, I know
    They are friends that come and go.
    But you and I are friends who stay
    Together."

Together we visit my tree of pine.
Together we talk to the four winds,
And listen to their secrets.
And sometimes the Witch Wind
Shrieks and hollers and blows to us.
And together we hear old neighbor owl call, "Who?"
And we call back, "Here we are!
Where are you?"

"A Prayer of Thanks"

Thank you, Great Cat, who has made the world with
  your silken paws.
Thank you, Witch Wind, for Who.

I will always love my four winds,
And the far-singing stars,
And neighbor owl,
And the sky-lighting moon…

...and my tree of pine.

Mark Taylor

Professionally Mark Taylor has been a librarian, a coordinator of radio programs for children, the star of a weekly, half-hour television program for children, a reviewer of children's books, an author of textbooks and a teacher of children's literature. By avocation he is a harpist, guitarist, folk singer, folklorist, linguist, and ballet dancer. He is widely known as a storyteller. It is this talent, and a keen ear for the poetry of words, that he puts to work in this book. Other books include, *Henry the Explorer, Henry Explores the Jungle,* and *Henry the Castaway.*

Erik Blegvad

Erik Blegvad was born in Copenhagen, Denmark, and he studied at the School of Applied Arts there. He came to the United States in 1951 and has since illustrated many children's books and magazine articles. He also taught illustration at the School of Visual Arts in New York City. He now lives in London.